For the Teacher

This reproducible study guide consists of instructional material to use in conjunction with the novel *The Adventures of Tom Sawyer*. Written in chapter-by-chapter format, the guide contains a synopsis, pre-reading activities, vocabulary and comprehension exercises, as well as extension activities to be used as follow-up to the novel.

NOVEL-TIES are either for whole class instruction using a single title or for group instruction where each group uses a different novel appropriate to its reading level. Depending upon the amount of time allotted to it in the classroom, each novel, with its guide and accompanying lessons, may be completed in two to four weeks.

The first step in using NOVEL-TIES is to distribute to each student a copy of the novel and a folder containing all of the duplicated worksheets. Begin instruction by selecting several pre-reading activities in order to set the stage for the reading ahead. Vocabulary exercises for each chapter always precede the reading so that new words will be reinforced in the context of the book. Use the questions on the chapter worksheets for class discussion or as written exercises.

The benefits of using NOVEL-TIES are numerous. Students read good literature in the original, rather than in abridged or edited form. The good reading habits formed by practice in focusing on interpretive comprehension and literary techniques will be transferred to the books students read independently. Passive readers become active, avid readers.

Novel-Ties® are printed on recycled paper.

SYNOPSIS

The Adventures of Tom Sawyer, one of the great classics of American literature, relates the experiences of a boy living in the small town of St. Petersburg on the Mississippi River in the early nineteenth century. The picture of a boyhood in that time and place, as painted by the author, is almost idyllic. It calls to mind freedom from constraints, from hypocrisy, and from responsibility; and a devotion only to adventure, excitement, and the simple joys of playtime and fantasy.

We first meet Tom in his typical pursuit of playing hooky from school and outfoxing his Aunt Polly, with whom he lives. This time, however, he is "squealed on" by his half-brother Sid and is assigned the task of whitewashing the fence the next day. With youthful ingeniousness, Tom transforms the punishment into a social triumph for himself by making it seem both appealing and unavailable to his friends. They soon line up and barter their greatest treasures for an "opportunity" to whitewash.

Tom's next challenge appears in the form of Becky Thatcher, a pretty, demure girl newly arrived in St. Petersburg with her mother and father, the venerated Judge Thatcher. Instantly forgetting his former love for Amy Lawrence, Tom begins a frenzied courtship with Becky, which mostly takes the form of "showing off" at her house, in church, and at school. On the verge of conquest, Tom makes the mistake of mentioning his earlier "engagement" to Amy; the romance is suddenly destroyed, and Tom and Becky experience jealousy, spite, and misery before they are reunited.

Meanwhile, Tom keeps a midnight appointment with Huckleberry Finn, a town vagrant his own age, at the graveyard. There they witness the murder of Dr. Robinson, who has hired two miscreants, Injun Joe and Muff Potter, to help him steal a body for medical research. Although Joe commits the deed, he sets up Muff Potter as the murderer. Potter was drunk and unconscious at the time and takes the blame with little protest; in the entire village the only ones who know the truth are Tom and Huck. Out of fear of Injun Joe, the two boys take an oath never to reveal the truth.

These two plots, one a romance and the other a mystery, proceed side by side through many adventures. Tom attends his own funeral after a pirating adventure. He takes Becky's whipping at school when she accidentally tears the master's book. Guilty for not revealing the truth about the murder, Tom later testifies at Muff Potter's trial. Finally, Huck and Tom search for buried treasure.

At this point in the novel, the plots begin to merge. Tom and Huck secretly witness a disguised Injun Joe discover a treasure box and determine to follow him to learn where he has hidden it. Huck watches over Injun Joe, while Tom attends a picnic with Becky during which they become lost in the labryinths of McDougal's cave. Tom proves his courage during the long ordeal and finally succeeds in finding a way out. To prevent anyone else from becoming lost inside, Judge Thatcher locks the door to the cave. When Tom announces that Injun Joe is inside, the villagers rush to discover his starved corpse behind the door.

In the final adventure, Tom and Huck successfully play their hunch that the treasure is in the cave. The two boys become rich, and heroes as well. Huck soon comes to regret his new wealth because it means becoming civilized, but a now somewhat-more-mature yet still-boyish Tom offers him membership in the soon-to-be-formed Tom Sawyer's Gang if Huck will be respectable. The book ends with the reader assuming that the adventures go on, as in fact they do in Twain's sequel and masterpiece, *The Adventures of Huckleberry Finn.*

AUTHOR INFORMATION

Samuel Langhorne Clemens, the American humorist and novelist, was born on November 30, 1835, in Florida, Missouri. When he was four years old the family moved to Hannibal, Missouri, a fast growing town on the Mississippi River, from which he drew many of his fictional characters, and which he renamed St. Petersburg in his books.

Clemens was only eleven when his father died. A year later he quit school to become an apprentice printer to his brother Orion. He learned to set type and correct copy; he also read most of the English classics. He later worked as a newspaperman in Philadelphia and New York, reporting primarily on politics. Disillusioned, he characterized politicians as having "the smallest minds and the selfishest souls and the cowardliest hearts that God makes."

Clemens left reporting to return to Missouri and become an apprentice to Horace Bixby, a Mississippi steamboat pilot. He loved the itinerant life and the opportunity to observe people. After four years on the river, he left to fight briefly with the Confederate army during the War between the States, although he did not approve of slavery.

At the age of twenty-seven he went back to newspaper work, adopting the pen name Mark Twain, a term used by riverboat pilots to mean "two fathoms deep: safe water." Skillfully blending caricature, homespun humor, and political irony, he grew from a newspaper humorist into a social satirist.

In 1865, Twain published his sketch, "Jim Smiley and His Jumping Frog" (later renamed "The Celebrated Jumping Frog of Calaveras County"). This became an overnight success and Twain's career was launched. He married Olivia Langdon in 1870 and, in 1871 they moved to Hartford, Connecticut, his home for the most productive and prosperous years of his life. Over the next twenty years he published such books as *Roughing It* (1872), *The Golden Age* (1873), *The Adventures of Tom Sawyer* (1876), *A Tramp Abroad* (1880), *The Prince and the Pauper* (1882), *Life on the Mississippi* (1883), *The Adventures of Huckleberry Finn* (1884), and *A Connecticut Yankee in King Arthur's Court* (1889).

Twain lost most of his fortune by investing in a typesetting machine which proved to be a costly failure. In order to pay his debts, he was forced to undertake a lecture tour at the age of sixty which ruined his health, but did, with the publication of three new books (*Pudd'nhead Wilson, Personal Recollections of Joan of Arc,* and *Following the Equator*), help to re-establish his fortune.

The last fifteen years of Twain's life brought personal tragedies and increased professional recognition. Two of his three daughters, his wife, and his brother Orion died. He received honorary degrees from Yale University, the University of Missouri, and Oxford University, England. Before he died at his home in Redding, Connecticut in 1910, Mark Twain had established himself as a prominent man of letters.

BACKGROUND INFORMATION

Twain was the first American writer to accurately portray his own real-life experiences in a novel. He drew his characters and the setting for *The Adventures of Tom Sawyer* directly from Hannibal, Missouri, population 500. Here are some known examples of relationships between Twain's fictional creations and people he really knew:

Character	Source
Tom Sawyer	a combination of several boys with whom Clemens was familiar, including himself
Huck Finn	Tom Blankenship, a boyhood friend
Widow Douglas	Mrs. Haliday, a widow in Hannibal
Aunt Polly	Clemens's mother
Jim	Uncle Dan'l, an African-American slave

PRE-READING ACTIVITIES

1. Read the Author Information on page two of this study guide and do some additional research on the life of Samuel Clemens, a.k.a. Mark Twain. Learn how Twain used the setting and incidents of his childhood as inspiration for *The Adventures of Tom Sawyer*.

2. **Social Studies Connection:** Locate Hannibal, Missouri on a map. Notice its proximity to the Mississippi River. Do some research to learn about life in a rural town along the Mississippi in the years prior to the Civil War. How did the active steamboat trade affect the lives of those who lived along the river?

3. The techniques of satire, burlesque, and cynicism all play an important role in Twain's writing style.
   - satire   the use of ridicule, irony, or sarcasm for the purpose of exposing human vice or folly
   - burlesque   a literary, dramatic, or other imitation which makes a caricature of that which it represents
   - cynicism   an attitude of contemptuous distrust of human nature and its motives

   Have you ever encountered these devices in literature or in film? As you read *Tom Sawyer* fill in a chart, such as the one below, to record examples of satire, burlesque, and cynicism. You will notice that these devices are used most effectively when Twain describes adults; his tone toward young people is tempered by tolerant understanding and quiet amusement.

Elements of Style	Examples
satire	
burlesque	
cynicism	

4. Have you ever seen a film or read a book in which two or more plots are intertwined? How did the plots converge? The two main plots of this novel are a love story and a mystery story. Tom's character provides the transition from one to the other. As you read, notice Twain's skill as a storyteller as he deftly intertwines all the elements of this tale.

5. Obtain copies of Alexander Dumas's book *The Man in the Iron Mask* as well as works by Sir Walter Scott. Tom used these popular adventure stories as a basis for his imaginative games. Read several passages from these books for their language and flavor before you begin reading *The Adventures of Tom Sawyer*.

Pre-Reading Activities (cont.)

6. Do some research to learn about "dime-store" novels, a popular new form of literature in the mid-nineteenth century. Typically, the hero saves the heroine from the clutches of a villain, and the writer ends his chapter with a "cliffhanger" in order to build suspense and sustain the reader's interest. Tom Sawyer contains many scenes which are burlesques of these literary styles. As you read, look for scenes of melodrama, mistaken identity, or unlikely coincidence, all of which illustrate Twain's talent for tongue-in-cheek mockery.

7. Conduct a classroom survey to find out if any of your classmates are superstitous. If so, make a list of commonly held superstitions. As you read, compare the superstitions on this list with those of Tom and his contemporaries.

8. Much of *The Adventures of Tom Sawyer* was written in the vernacular; that is, the language commonplace at the time and in the location represented in the novel, but not necessarily used in standard English. For example:

   - There was a slight noise behind her and she turned in time to seize a small boy by the slack of his <u>roundabout</u> and arrest his flight.

   - And look at your mouth. What is that <u>truck</u>?

   - He plans to know just how long he can torment me before I get my <u>dander up</u>, . . .

   - . . . I've *got* to do some of my duty by him, or I'll be the <u>ruination</u> of the child.

   - . . . I bet you I'll <u>lam</u> Sid for that. I'll learn him!

   - . . . when he climbed cautiously in at the window he uncovered an <u>ambuscade</u>, in the person of his aunt.

   Keep a list of these expressions as you read the novel. Define as many as possible through context; use a standard dictionary or a dictionary of slang if necessary. Why do you think Twain wrote in the vernacular?

9. **Literary Element—Characterization:** Begin a character chart, such as the one below, listing personality traits of each character. Add to it as new characters are introduced. As you read, consider why some critics have said that Twain's portraits are caricatures rather than characters.

Character	Personality Traits
Tom	
Huck	
Aunt Polly	

PREFACE, CHAPTERS 1 – 3

Vocabulary: Synonyms are words with similar meanings. Draw a line from each word in column A to its synonym in column B. Then use the words in column A to fill in the blanks in the sentences below.

A		B	
1.	guile	a.	desire
2.	sagacity	b.	scorn
3.	derision	c.	begging
4.	alacrity	d.	fleeting
5.	covet	e.	deceit
6.	intrepid	f.	sullen
7.	evanescent	g.	eagerness
8.	pliant	h.	wisdom
9.	morose	i.	fearless
10.	beseeching	j.	flexible

· ·

1. It is easier to walk in a shoe with a(n) _________________ sole than one with a stiff, heavy sole.

2. It is better to be satisfied with what you have than to _________________ your neighbor's wealth.

3. The bank teller's _________________ was not discovered until a large sum of money was found missing from the bank.

4. The _________________ of her classmates caused the newcomer to avoid school.

5. After a series of personal tragedies, my friend became _________________ and bitter.

6. The _________________ pilot flew his plane despite warnings of a severe storm.

7. Knowing that he would please his audience, the magician performed with _________________.

8. Understanding that the joy of his victory was a(n) _________________ experience, the athlete tried to enjoy the moment.

9. Admired for his _________________, the elder's advice was sought by everyone in the village.

10. Stranded with a flat tire, the woman cast _________________ glances to all who passed by.

Preface, Chapters 1 – 3 (cont.)

Questions:

1. According to the Preface, why does Twain want adults as well as children to read this book?

2. What evidence proves that Tom visited the swimming hole? Who points this out to Aunt Polly?

3. How does Tom enteratin himself after supper?

4. How does Tom avoid whitewashing the fence?

5. How does Tom acquire his new-found wealth? What are some articles in his new collection of treasures?

6. What is Twain's definition of "work" and "play"?

7. How does Tom take his revenge on Sid?

8. How does Tom show his "love" for the new girl he sees? How does she return his attentions?

9. What causes Tom to sink into a depressed state of mind? How does Tom's imagination increase his sorrow?

Questions for Discussion:

1. Why do you think Tom "shows off" so much? Do you think Twain is being critical of Tom's personality?

2. The episode of Tom whitewashing the fence is one of the most famous scenes in American literature. Discuss what makes his scene so interesting from these perspectives:

   - psychological

   - humorous

   - cultural–revealing certain typical elements of the boys' level of maturity and the time and place in which it occurred.

   Can you think of any other scenes from books that you have read that are as memorable and carry as much insight as this one?

Preface, Chapters 1 – 3 (cont.)

Literary Devices:

I. *Oxymoron*—An oxymoron is a figure of speech in which contradictory or incongruous terms are combined, usually for emphasis. The word "oxymoron" comes from the combination of two Greek word parts: *oxys* meaning "sharp" + *moros* meaning dull and is itself an oxymoron. Some examples of oxymorons are:

- bitterly happy
- open secret
- original copy
- down escalator

Find at least two oxymorons in Chapter Three.

_______________________________   _______________________________

Think of two other oxymorons and write them below.

_______________________________   _______________________________

II. *Simile*—A simile is a comparison of two unlike objects using the words "like" or "as." For example, when Tom and the new boy are fighting in Chapter One, they "gripped together like cats."

What does this simile suggest about the boys' activity?

____

Return to the text to find the simile used to suggest the behavior of the new boy at the end of the fight.

____

____

III. *Metaphor*—A metaphor is an implied or suggesed comparison. For example:

> [Tom] compared the insignificant whitewashed streak with the far-reaching continent of unwhitewashed fence.

What is the fence compared to?

____

Why do you think this comparison is made?

____

____

Writing Activity:

Imagine that you are the new girl and see Tom Sawyer in front of your house. What do you think of him? Write a journal entry as if you were that girl.

CHAPTERS 4 – 8

Vocabulary: Synonyms are words with similar meanings. Draw a line from each word in column A to its synonym in column B. Then use the words in column A to fill in the blanks in the sentences below.

<u>A</u>		<u>B</u>	
1.	disconcerted	a.	gushing
2.	éclat	b.	think
3.	mien	c.	perturbed
4.	effusion	d.	appearance
5.	pariah	e.	outcast
6.	facetious	f.	sparkle
7.	zephyr	g.	breeze
8.	cogitate	h.	humorous

. . . .

1. The conductor became ___________________ when the violins played off-key.

2. Unlike those who are quick to draw conclusions, I must always ___________________ and then talk to others before I make a decision.

3. I became a(n) ___________________ in my own club once I challenged the decision of our president.

4. Dressed in a jacket and tie, my father had such an elegant ___________________ that he was never mistaken for a farmer.

5. The pianist gave a performance of such great ___________________ that the entire audience rose to applaud.

6. The innkeeper greeted his guests with a(n) ___________________ of smiles, hand-shakes, and other gestures to make them feel welcome.

7. I realized that my ___________________ remark had been taken seriously when no one laughed.

8. As the ___________________ blew across the desk, it cooled our bodies, making us feel comfortable on a scorching day.

Chapters 4 – 8 (cont.)

Word Study:

The word "benediction," which means "the blessing at the end of a church service," comes from two Latin words: *bene* meaning "well" and *dict* meaning "tell" or "say." Fill in the chart below using your knowledge of the word roots *bene* and *dict*. When you have finished you may use a dictionary to add several words of your own.

Word	Meaning
benefit	
benefactor	
benevolent	
benign	
diction	
predict	
verdict	
contradict	
dictate	
dictator	
malediction	

Questions:

1. Why is Tom presented with a Bible? Do you think he deserved to get it?

2. Why is Judge Thatcher especially important to Tom?

3. How does Twain satirize the "young clerks" in church?

4. How does Tom's pinch-bug liven up the church service?

5. Why do all the boys in town envy Huck Finn?

6. What three methods to cure warts are discussed by Tom and Huck?

7. Why does Tom purposely invite punishment for his tardiness to school?

8. How does Tom's wooing of Becky employ certain rituals typical of their era?

Questions for Discussion:

Do you believe in any superstitions? If so, what are they? How does Twain make fun of superstition?

Chapters 4 – 8 (cont.)

Literary Devices:

I. *Simile and Metaphor*—Read the first paragraph of Chapter Four carefully. How does Twain use simile and metaphor to create the images of a church building and a church service? Which words refer to a building?

____

____

____

Which words refer to a church service?

____

____

II. *Irony*—Irony is used by a writer to express something opposite from what is expected. What is ironic about the award of the Bible that was given to Tom?

____

Find other examples of Twain's use of irony in Chapters Four and Five.

____

____

____

____

III. *Personification*—Personification is a figure of speech in which an author grants human qualities to nonhuman objects. For example:

Nature lay in a trance.

What is being personified?

____

____

What mood does this create?

____

____

Writing Activity:

Write about a time when you or someone you know created mischief in an institutional setting, such as a school or church. Describe the act of mischief and tell why it was inappropriate in its setting. Did punishment result from the action? If so, was it fairly or unfairly administered?

CHAPTERS 9 – 17

Vocabulary: Draw a line from each word on the left to its definition on the right. Then answer the questions below.

1.	lugubrious	a.	in a secretive way; deceptively
2.	miscreant	b.	mournful; gloomy
3.	clandestinely	c.	uneasy; fearful
4.	purloined	d.	depraved, villainous individual
5.	soliloquized	e.	lacking in variety; boring
6.	monotonous	f.	uttered to oneself
7.	pallid	g.	lacking in color; pale
8.	apprehensive	h.	taken dishonestly; stolen

. . . .

1. In what situation would you expect to hear a <u>lugubrious</u> wail?

   ____

   ____

2. How might a <u>miscreant</u> be treated by the law?

   ____

   ____

3. How might an instructor prevent his lectures from becoming <u>monotonous</u>?

   ____

   ____

4. For what reasons might people wish to meet <u>clandestinely</u>?

   ____

   ____

5. Under what circumstances at school might you become <u>apprehensive</u>?

   ____

   ____

6. Why would its owner be upset about a <u>purloined</u> dog?

   ____

   ____

7. What activities might change your complexion from <u>pallid</u> to one with a healthy glow?

   ____

   ____

8. Who would be listening to a <u>soliloquized</u> statement?

   ____

   ____

Chapters 9 – 17 (cont.)

Word Study:

The word "audible" comes from the Latin *audire*, "to hear." How are the following words related to *audire*? The first one has been done for you.

Word	Meaning	Relation to *Audire*
auditorium	large room where people assemble	place where something is heard
audit		
audition		
audio		
audiologist		

Questions:

1. Why do Tom and Huck take an oath in the graveyard?

2. What does Aunt Polly do to Tom that is worse than a whipping?

3. What do Tom and Huck expect will happen to Injun Joe as he relates his version of the murder? What is their explanation when nothing happens?

4. Why does Tom feel guilty about Muff Potter?

5. How does Aunt Polly's behavior poke fun at some of the medical practices of her time?

6. How does Peter, the cat, teach Aunt Polly a lesson?

7. Why does Tom resolve to run away? Why does Joe Harper join him?

8. Why is there a ferry on the river?

9. Why do Joe and Tom have to hunt for Joe's "lost knife"?

10. What act of nature tests the boys' ability to survive?

11. According to Tom, what is "the proudest moment of his life"?

Chapters 9 – 17 (cont.)

Questions for Discussion:

1. Why do you think Twain called the young "pirates" Tom and Joe "curiously inconsistent"?

2. Would you characterize Tom as being primarily evil, mischievous, or kind-hearted? What examples from the novel back up your conclusion?

Literary Element: Characterization

Use the Venn diagram below to compare the characters of Tom and Huck. Write about their similar qualities in the overlapping part of the circles. Add information to the diagram as you continue to read the book.

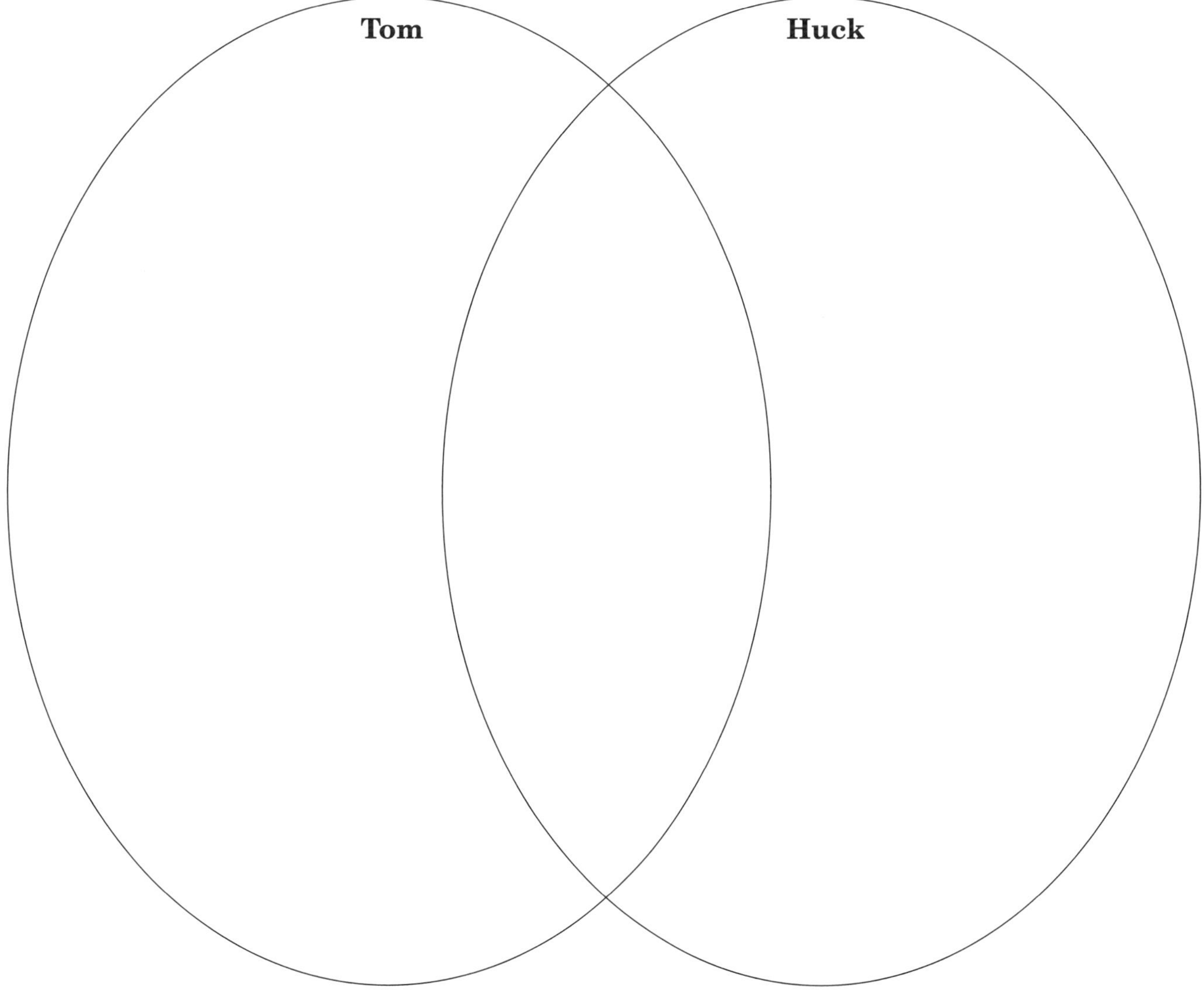

Chapters 9 – 17 (cont.)

Literary Devices:

I. *Comic Relief*—Comic relief is the insertion of a comic element into a serious work. Its purpose is to relieve the tension and to broaden the scope of the work by contrasting the humorous with the tragic. How does Chapter Twelve provide comic relief from the events preceding it?

____

____

____

II. *Dramatic Irony*—Dramatic irony, a device used more often in plays than in novels, refers to a situation in which the reader or a member of the audience, understands something of which another character is innocent. In what way is Aunt Polly's assessment of Tom after his "death" an example of dramatic irony?

____

____

____

Writing Activity:

One of Twain's greatest strengths as a writer is his portrayal of human nature and behavior. Write a well-organized essay using examples from Chapter Seventeen to illustrate how accurately Twain captures human behavior before, during, and after Tom's "funeral."

CHAPTERS 18 – 21

Vocabulary: Use the context to determine the meaning of the underlined word in each of the following sentences. Compare your definition with a dictionary definition.

1. We were warned to <u>refrain</u> from drinking our tap water because it may have become polluted after the flood.

2. Once the weather turned cool, the <u>lethargy</u> we felt during the hot, humid days ended.

3. Never expect an apology from my brother who is known to be a <u>vindictive</u> person.

4. After working in the hot sun for hours, we walked home <u>languidly</u>.

5. I took a special course to learn what I should do in case I <u>encounter</u> a storm when I am out at sea.

6. I prefer to wear dark clothes rather than brightly colored attired so that I won't be <u>conspicuous</u> in a crowd.

7. The new arrivals to our country gazed in <u>perplexity</u> at the directions on the signs.

8. Light from the chandelier reflected on the bald man's <u>pate</u>.

Word	Your Definition	Dictionary Definition
1. refrain		
2. lethargy		
3. vindictive		
4. languidly		
5. encounter		
6. conspicuous		
7. perplexity		
8. pate		

Chapters 18 – 21 (cont.)

Questions:

1. Why is Aunt Polly upset with Tom even after she knows he's alive?

2. How does Tom shock Aunt Polly into giving him a special apple she had been "saving for him"?

3. Why does Becky choose to invite friends to a picnic?

4. Why does Alfred ruin a page of Tom's spelling book? Why doesn't Becky come to Tom's rescue?

5. Why does Aunt Polly say she could forgive Tom for "a million sins"?

6. How does Tom's impulsive nature further his romance with Becky?

7. How do the boys take revenge on Mr. Dobbins?

Questions for Discussion:

1. In what ways does Tom show that he is resourceful? When have you needed to be resourceful in your own life?

2. Do you think that Aunt Polly should have suspected Tom's dream? Why do you think she is so gullible?

3. In your opinion are any of Tom's "lies" justified?

4. In what ways are Tom's school experiences different from your experiences in school today?

5. Have you ever overheard a conversation about yourself as Tom did when he eavesdropped on the people mourning his "death"? If the opportunity arose, would you risk the possibility of overhearing criticism?

6. In your opinion, do you think Twain wanted you to sympathize with the boys' prank against the school master? Did it seem cruel or mischievous to you?

Chapters 18 – 21 (cont.)

Literary Element: Characterization

Use the chart below to record examples of times when Tom and Becky showed the following list of emotions.

Emotion	Tom	Becky
jealousy		
vanity		
forced gaiety		
revenge		
frustration		
impatience		
misery		

Literary Devices:

I. *Personification*—What is being personified in the following passage?

> A whole hour drifted by, the master nodding in his throne,
> the air was drowsy with the hum of study.

What atmosphere does this passage create?

II. *Satire*—Why do you think Twain satirizes young women's commencement speeches? What aspects of these speeches does he ridicule?

Chapters 18 – 21 (cont.)

III. *Allusion*—Allusion in literature is a reference to a familiar person, place, or event.

> [The commencement recital] was the most eloquent thing he had
> ever listened to, and that Daniel Webster himself might well be
> proud of it.

Who was Daniel Webster, and why might he have been proud of a speech?

____

____

____

3 – 2 – 1 Summary:

Use the 3 – 2 – 1 format to summarize these chapters.

3 Plot elements that are still unresolved

____

____

____

2 Emotions of Aunt Polly

____

____

1 Reason the boys want to get revenge on Mr. Dobbins

____

Writing Activity:

Twain often presents action as if he were writing scenes in a play. For example, Chapter
Eighteen seems to be written in two acts: Aunt Polly's house and the school house. Choose
either of these scenes, or any other scene you choose and write dialogue for it. After it is
written, ask several classmates to help you dramatize your scene.

CHAPTERS 22 – 29

Vocabulary: Draw a line from each word on the left to its definition on the right. Then use the numbered words to fill in the blanks in the sentences below.

1.	stolid	a.	infinitely wise; all knowing
2.	omniscient	b.	acquired
3.	auspices	c.	impassive; not easily excited
4.	palpable	d.	shifts back and forth
5.	attrition	e.	wearing down; gradual loss
6.	procured	f.	constant; habitual
7.	fluctuates	g.	patronage; sponsorship
8.	chronic	h.	easily seen; obvious

. . . .

1. A notice in the program indicated that the play came to this theater under the
    ____________________ of our local Chamber of Commerce.

2. After much persuasion, I____________________ an antique dresser from a family that
    really did not want to sell it.

3. We packed a heavy coat and a bathing suit in our suitcase because the weather
    ____________________ between cold and hot.

4. The ____________________ expressions of the jurors did not reveal their verdict.

5. I did not go to the doctor until the occasional pain in my back became
    ____________________.

6. Rather than firing all of their older employees, the company decided to thin their
    ranks by ____________________.

7. Many religions worship one ____________________ being.

8. We knew the boy's statement that he had been at school was a(n) ____________________
    lie because we saw him at the movie theater.

Etymology: Words From Names

During Tom's listless summer days, a mesmerizer comes to town. The word
mesmerizer comes from the name of Franz Anton Mesmer (1734–1815), an Austrian
physician, who treated patients with hypnotism. Use a dictionary or go online to
find out about the people from whom these words are derived:

- boycott
- braille
- curie
- diesel
- Fahrenheit
- leotard
- pasteurize
- sandwich
- silhouette

Chapters 22 – 29 (cont.)

Questions:

1. Why does Tom think his summer is getting off to a terrible start?

2. Why do Tom and Huck suffer guilt when Muff Potter praises their good treatment of him?

3. Why does Tom suffer feelings of insecurity after the trial?

4. Why do Tom and Huck begin digging holes in several places in town?

5. How is it revealed that Tom and Huck's spirit of adventure has overcome fear?

6. Why do Tom and Huck change their plans concerning the haunted house? What do they do instead?

7. Why are Injun Joe and his companion glad they had come to the haunted house?

8. Why do Tom and Huck decide to track down Injun Joe?

9. Why is Tom pleased when Judge Thatcher returns to town?

10. Why is Injun Joe planning an act of revenge against Widow Douglas?

11. Why doesn't Huck go along with the plan to inform Tom when Injun Joe returns?

Questions for Discussion:

1. Do you agree with Tom that to promise *not* to do a thing is "the surest way in the world to make a body want to go and do that very thing"? Have you or anyone you know ever felt this way?

2. Why do you think Twain did not have the reader "witness" Tom's pre-trial visit to Muff's lawyer?

3. In what ways does this book reflect the open prejudice that existed against minorities at the time this book portrayed?

4. What do you think Tom's and Huck's plans to do with their part of the treasure reveals about each of them?

5. In what ways does superstition direct the lives of Tom and Huck? Do you have any superstitions that affect your behavior?

Drama Connection:

Dramatize the court scene in which Muff Potter is tried for murder. Use your own words to add to the dialogue already provided by Twain and have the prosecutor question each witness. Act out the scene to the point where Injun Joe crashes through the window.

Chapters 22 – 29 (cont.)

Literary Device: Cliffhanger

A cliffhanger is a device borrowed from serialized silent films in which an episode ends at a moment of suspense. In a book it usually appears at the end of a chapter to encourage the reader to go on in the book. What is the cliffhanger at the end of Chapter XXVI?

____

____

What is the cliffhanger at the end of Chapter XXIX?

____

____

Writing Activities:

1. Twain ridicules superstition and the role it plays in people's lives. Write about the ways superstition adds to the novel in terms of development of character and plot. You may want to add a discussion of superstitions that people believe in today.

2. Write about a real or imagined time when you overheard a conversation that was not meant for you to hear. Describe what you learned and tell how you acted upon the information.

CHAPTERS 30 – 35

Vocabulary: Use the context to determine the meaning of the underlined words in each of the following sentences. Then compare your definition with one you find in a dictionary.

1. As thick clouds formed over the lake, the people in the sailboat felt a <u>boding</u> uneasiness.

   Your definition ____

   Dictionary definition ____

2. The <u>lucid</u> instructions on the kit made the model easy to assemble.

   Your definition ____

   Dictionary definition ____

3. It was easy to lose one's direction in the <u>sinuous</u> passageways of the cave.

   Your definition ____

   Dictionary definition ____

4. The two children divided the sandwich in half and each one ate his <u>moiety</u>.

   Your definition ____

   Dictionary definition ____

5. The abandoned puppy was a <u>forlorn</u> figure sitting out in the rain.

   Your definition ____

   Dictionary definition ____

6. The play was so <u>insipid</u> that many people in the audience fell asleep.

   Your definition ____

   Dictionary definition ____

7. Even though I offered a <u>plausible</u> excuse for my lateness, everyone thought I had just overslept.

   Your definition ____

   Dictionary definition ____

8. We were able to escape those who pursued us by ducking down into the <u>subterranean</u> passage that let us out two miles from where we started.

   Your definition ____

   Dictionary definition ____

Chapters 30 – 35 (cont.)

Questions:

1. How does Tom show maturity and responsibility during the crisis in the cave?

2. Why does Tom panic when he learns that the entrance to the cave has been sealed off?

3. Why does Tom experience mixed emotions upon seeing Injun Joe dead?

4. Why does Tom want Huck to go back into the cave with him?

5. In what ways is Tom more prepared for cave exploring the second time? Why does Tom take along little bags?

6. How does Sid once again show his mean nature?

7. How does Tom upstage the widow's surprise?

8. Why does Huck run away form the Widow Douglas?

9. How does Tom entice Huck back to civilization?

Questions for Discussion:

1. Do you think Injun Joe deserved a funeral ceremony? What do you think Twain was saying about the people in the community?

2. Which do you think more accurately conveyed Tom's character—his treatment of Becky in the cave, or his proposed treatment of women if he became a robber?

3. Do you think the Widow Douglas and Aunt Polly managed the boys' money in the best possible way?

4. Do you think there is any merit to Huck's criticism of civilized life? Would any of his criticisms apply to life today?

Literary Devices:

I. *Dramatic Irony*—How is the Welshman's statement to Tom and Huck upon seeing them hauling their bags of treasure an example of dramatic irony?

> . . . the boys in this town will take more trouble and fool away
> more time hunting up six bits' worth of iron to sell to the foundry
> than they would to make twice the money at regular work.

____

____

____

Chapters 30 – 35 (cont.)

II. *Personification*—What is being personified in the following passage:

> The children fastened their eyes upon their bit of candle and
> watched it melt slowly and pitilessly away; saw the half inch
> of wick stand alone at last; saw the feeble flame rise and fall,
> climb the thin column of smoke, linger at its top a moment,
> and then—the horror of utter darkness reigned!

Why is this better than just saying, "The children saw the last bit of their candle go
out, leaving them in the dark"?

Science Connection:

Do some research to learn about caves and spelunking, the act of exploring caves. Find
pictures of caves and of stalagmites and stalactites, the limestone formations that appear
in some caves.

Writing Activities:

1. Imagine you are a TV news reporter interviewing Tom and Huck. Write their responses
   to your questions about their childhood, the recent wealth that has come their way,
   and their plans for the future.

2. As readers we do not witness Tom and Becky leaving the cave: it is only reported.
   Pretend that you are either Tom or Becky and write a journal entry describing your
   experiences in the cave and your escape.

CLOZE ACTIVITY

The following excerpt is taken directly from Chapter Fifteen. Read it through completely and then fill in the blanks with words that make sense. Afterwards, you may compare your language with that of the author.

He went on listening, and gathered by odds and ends that it was conjectured at first that the boys had got drowned while taking a swim; then the ______________ [1] raft had been missed; next, certain boys ______________ [2] the missing lads had promised that the ______________ [3] should "hear something" soon; the wiseheads had "______________ [4] this and that together" and decided that ______________ [5] lads had gone off on that raft ______________ [6] would turn up at the next town ______________, [7] presently; but toward noon the raft had ______________ [8] found, lodged against the Missouri shore some ______________ [9] or six miles below the village—and ______________ [10] hope perished; they must be drowned, else ______________ [11] would have driven them home by nightfall ______________ [12] not sooner. It was believed that the ______________ [13] for the bodies had been a fruitless ______________ [14] merely because the drowning must have occurred ______________ [15] mid-channel, since the boys, being good swimmers, ______________ [16] otherwise have escaped to shore. This was ______________ [17] night. If the bodies continued missing until ______________, [18] all hope would be given over and ______________ [19] funerals would be preached on that morning. ______________ [20] shuddered.

Mrs. Harper gave a sobbing good ______________ [21] and turned to go. Then with a ______________ [22] impulse the two bereaved women flung themselves ______________ [23] each other's arms and had a good, ______________ [24] cry, and then parted. Aunt Polly was ______________ [25] far beyond her wont, in her good ______________ [26] to Sid and Mary. Sid snuffled a ______________ [27] and Mary went off crying with all ______________ [28] heart.

Aunt Polly knelt down and prayed for Tom so touchingly, so appealing, and with such measureless love in her words and her old trembling voice, that he was weltering in tears long before she was through.

POST-READING ACTIVITIES

1. Return to the Character Chart that you began in the Pre-Reading Activities on page three of this study guide. Add character names and personality traits to the chart. Compare your responses with those of your classmates and discuss whether these characters are realistic, caricatures, or both.

2. **Pair/Share:** Return to the chart on "Elements of Style—satire, burlesque, cynicism" that you began in the Pre-Reading Activities on page four of this study guide. Work with a partner to add examples of each element. Then compare your responses to those of others in your class.

3. Return to the Venn diagram that you began on page four of this study guide. Add information now that you have finished the novel.

4. Which of the following adjectives could be used to describe Tom? Choose three from the list below and briefly cite an incident from the story to illustrate each quality.

    - optimistic
    - courageous
    - affectionate
    - malicious
    - spiteful
    - uncivilized
    - romantic
    - pragmatic
    - mischievous

    Choose one word from the above list to describe Huck Finn and one to describe Sid Sawyer. Cite an episode from the story as proof for each. Share your responses with others who have read *The Adventures of Tom Sawyer*.

5. As a burlesque novel, *The Adventures of Tom Sawyer* contains characters who, in addition to being themselves, act as caricatures for certain types of people we all know and recognize. Give a general description of the type of person Twain had in mind when he portrayed each of these characters:

    - Tom
    - Aunt Polly
    - Becky
    - Mr. Dobbins
    - Sid
    - Injun Joe

6. **Symbolism:** A symbol in literature is a person, event, or object that represents an idea or a set of ideas.
    - How might the cave symbolize Tom's trial before he can reach maturity?
    - How might the treasure symbolize Tom's transition from childhood to young adulthood?

    What other examples of symbolism can you find in the novel?

7. **Plot:** The plot of a novel is its sequence of events and the order in which these events occur. *The Adventures of Tom Sawyer* has two important plot lines. How does Twain manage to merge the love plot and the murder plot? The climax refers to the most intense moment or the turning point of the plot. What do you think is the climax of each of the two plots?

Post-Reading Activities (cont.)

8. **Cooperative Learning Activity:** Work with a small cooperative learning group to discuss events in Tom's life that parallel those of your own even though the time and place may be distant. After your discussion, choose three situations that best point out the universal qualities of childhood as depicted by Mark Twain. Assign one group member the role of recorder to write about these three situations. Another group member can read them aloud to share with the other groups.

9. Use a Venn diagram, such as the one below, to compare your school with school in Tom's day. Write about their common characteristics in the overlapping part of the circles.

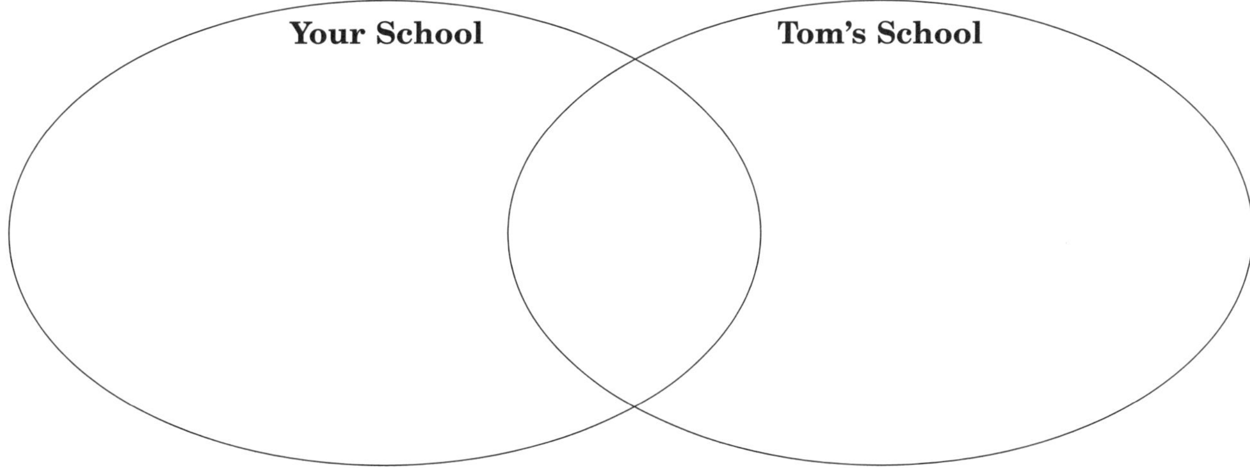

10. Imagine you have just found a lost chapter to *The Adventures of Tom Sawyer*. Write the adventure that befalls Tom in this hypothetical chapter.

11. Work with a small group of your classmates to choose and enact a scene from the book. Use as much of the existing dialogue from the book as possible.

12. **Cooperative Learning Activity:** Work with a group of your classmates to find one or more passages in the book that convey a strong message or are meaningful in some way. Present these passages to the other groups in your class and tell why they have been selected. Compare your selections with those chosen by other groups. Were there any passages that were chosen by more than one group?

13. **Fluency/Readers Theater:** Select a chapter from the book that has a lot of dialogue among several characters. Each character's dialogue should be read by one student. The characters should read only those words inside the quotation marks. Ignore phrases such as "he said" or "she said." One student can read the narration. Use simple props, such as hats, to identify the characters.

Post-Reading Activities (cont.)

14. **Pair/Share:** Hypocrisy is the pretense of having virtues that do not really exist. How does Twain point out the hypocrisy that exists in a small town, in its institutions, such as church and school, and among many of the characters introduced in the novel? Work with a partner to make a list of hypocrisies you have found in the book. Of what characters or institutions was Twain most critical? Do you think his criticisms were mainly heavy-handed or humorous?

15. **Literature Circle:** Have a literature circle discussion in which you tell your personal reactions to *The Adventures of Tom Sawyer*. Here are some questions and sentence starters to help your literature circle begin a discussion.
    * In what ways do you identify with Tom, Huck, or Becky?
    * Do you find the characters in the novel realistic even though they lived in the nineteenth century? Why or why not?
    * Which character did you like the most? The least?
    * Who else would you like to read this novel? Why?
    * If you could speak to Twain what would you ask him about this novel?
    * It was not fair when . . .
    * I would have liked to see . . .
    * I wonder . . .
    * Tom learned that . . .

SUGGESTIONS FOR FURTHER READING

Allen, Jerry. *The Adventures of Mark Twain*. Little, Brown.

Clemens, Samuel. *The Autobiography of Mark Twain*. Washington Square Press.

* Golding, William. *Lord of the Flies*. Putnam.

* Hinton, S.E. *The Outsiders*. Random House.

* Knowles, John. *A Separate Peace*. Random House.

* Lee, Harper. *To Kill a Mockingbird*. Warner Books.

* McGovern, Ann. *Robin Hood of Sherwood Forest*. Scholastic.

* Myers, Walter Dean. *Scorpions*. HarperCollins.

* Paterson, Katherine. *Bridge to Terabithia*. HarperCollins.

* Paulsen, Gary. *Hatchet*. Penguin.

* Peck, Robert. *Soup*. Random House.

* Rawls, Wilson. *Where the Red Fern Grows*. Random House.

* Steinbeck, John. *The Pearl*. Random House.

* _______________. *The Red Pony*. Random House.

* Swarthout, Glendon. *Bless the Beasts and Children*. Simon & Schuster.

* White, Robb. *Deathwatch*. Random House.

* Zindel, Paul. *The Pigman*. Random House.

Some Other Books by Mark Twain

* *The Adventures of Huckleberry Finn*. Random House.

A Connecticut Yankee in King Arthur's Court. New American Library.

Life on the Mississippi. New American Library.

The Prince and the Pauper. New American Library.

Pudd'nhead Wilson. New American Library.

* NOVEL-TIES Study Guides are available for these titles.

ANSWER KEY

Preface, Chapters 1 – 3

Vocabulary: 1. e 2. h 3. b 4. g 5. a 6. i 7. d 8. j 9. f 10. c; 1. pliant 2. covet 3. guile 4. derision 5. morose 6. intrepid 7. alacrity 8. evanescent 9. sagacity 10. beseeching

Questions: 1. Twain wants adults to read this book so that they will remember what it was like to be children. 2. Evidence that proves Tom visited the swimming hole is that he has black thread on his shirt collar instead of the white thread Aunt Polly had used. Sid, Tom's half-brother, points out this evidence to Aunt Polly. 3. After supper, Tom meets, beats up, and terrorizes the new boy in town as an after-dinner activity. 4. Tom avoids whitewashing the fence by making the job seem both appealing and unavailable to his friends: soon they are begging him for a chance to whitewash. 5. Tom's friends offer him their greatest treasures for a chance to paint. Some of these treasures include a kite, a dead rat on a string, blue bottle glass, twelve marbles, six firecrackers, and a brass doorknob. 6. According to Twain, "Work consists of whatever a body is obliged to do, and . . . Play consists of whatever a body is not obliged to do." 7. As revenge, Tom hurls a handful of "clods" (pieces of earth and grass) at Sid. 8. Tom reveals his "love" by glancing furtively at her for a while, then "showing off" with gymnastic feats to impress her. She rewards his attentions by throwing a pansy over the fence at him before going into the house. 9. Tom becomes depressed when Aunt Polly blames him for breaking the sugar bowl when Sid had actually done it; he feels he is wronged by her suspicions. He pictures himself dead and enjoys thinking of the sorrow this would cause Aunt Polly.

Chapters 4 – 8

Vocabulary: 1. c 2. f 3. d 4. a 5. e 6. h 7. g 8. b; 1. disconcerted 2. cogitate 3. pariah 4. mien 5. éclat 6. effusion 7. facetious 8. zephyr

Questions: 1. When Tom presents the correct number of "tickets" supposedly earned through Bible memorizations to the Reverend, he receives a Bible as a reward. Since Tom had actually bartered these "tickets" from his friends, it is hard to imagine he earned them in the conventional sense. 2. The great man visiting Sunday school is Judge Thatcher from nearby Constantinople. He turns out to be the father of the new girl in town whom Tom adores. 3. Twain satirizes the "young clerks" by describing them forming an "oiled and simpering" gauntlet through which the young women of the town have to pass and be inspected. 4. Tom lets the pinch-bug out of its box and it attacks a poodle who was wandering down the aisle in church. 5. The boys envy Huck because he lives with no restrictions; he is free to go where he wants, whenever he wants; he dresses as he pleases; and attends no school or church. All the children wish they dared to be like him. 6. According to Huck and Tom, warts may be cured by a dead cat, spunk-water in a stump, and a split bean. 7. Tom invites the punishment for tardiness because he knows he will be sent to sit with the girls; the only empty seat on the girls' side of the room is next to the new girl. 8. Tom and Becky's wooing employs shyness, showing off, male aggression, female coyness and eventual female surrender, and male pride.

Chapters 9 – 17

Vocabulary: 1. b 2. d 3. a 4. h 5. f 6. e 7. g 8. c; Answers to the second part of the vocabulary activity will vary.

Questions: 1. Tom and Huck witness the murder of Dr. Robinson by Injun Joe. They take an oath never to reveal that they witnessed the murder. 2. When Aunt Polly weeps over Tom and tells him he is breaking her heart, he considers this a punishment worse than a whipping. 3. Tom and Huck expect lightning to strike Injun Joe for lying. When nothing happens, they think that Joe must have sold himself to Satan who was protecting him. 4. When Muff Potter is accused of the murder, Tom feels guilty for knowing the truth and not speaking up. 5. Twain says of Aunt Polly, "She was one of those people who are infatuated with patent medicines and all newfangled methods of producing health or mending it." She unquestioningly follows any proposed remedy, whether it makes sense or not. 6. When the cat responds in agony to Tom's dose of Painkiller, Tom makes Aunt Polly realize that what may cause agony in a cat may do the same for a boy. 7. Tom feels unloved by both Aunt Polly and Becky and hopes they will be sorry when he is gone. Joe Harper's mother had punished him for drinking cream that he never tasted before, so he felt unloved and unwanted, too. 8. The ferry is being used to search for the supposedly dead bodies of Tom, Joe, and Huck. 9. Joe and Tom say they have to hunt for the knife because they feel sick from smoking, but won't admit it to each other or to Huck. 10. The act of nature that tests the boys is a tremendous thunder and lightning storm from which they must take cover under a huge oak tree. 11. The "proudest moment of his life" occurs as Tom walks down the church aisle at his own funeral, enjoying all the amazed looks being cast at him and hearing the fine things said about him.

Chapters 18 – 21

Vocabulary: 1. refrain–hold back   2. lethargy–sluggish indifference   3. vindictive–vengeful; unforgiving   4. languidly–lacking energy   5. encounter–come upon, meet with   6. conspicuous–easily seen; noticeable   7. perplexity–bewilderment   8. pate–top of the head

Questions: 1. Aunt Polly is upset thinking that Tom cared so little for her that he let her suffer while believing he was dead. 2. Tom shocks Aunt Polly into giving him the apple by telling her of the "dream" he had while pirating which relates the entire overheard conversation between her and Mrs. Harper when they thought their boys were dead. Aunt Polly believes this is a "vision" of Tom's. 3. Becky chooses to invite friends to a picnic to take revenge on Tom who is not paying any attention to her. 4. Feeling the need for revenge after he realized that Becky's attention to him only came about because she was trying to make Tom jealous, Alfred, in a fit of vengefulness, pours ink on a page of Tom's spelling book. Becky doesn't try to stop him, thereby rescuing Tom from their teacher's anger, because she, too, wants revenge against Tom. 5. Aunt Polly forgives Tom because she finds the piece of bark that Tom had told her about with his message for her. 6. Tom apologizes impulsively to Becky. Later Tom saves Becky the embarrassment of a whipping by confessing to her crime of tearing the pages in the master's book. This succeeds in winning her back. 7. The boys take revenge by painting Mr. Dobbins's bald head gold. While he is occupied at the blackboard, they suspend a cat on a string to remove his wig and reveal the gold head to the audience.

Chapters 22 – 29

Vocabulary: 1. c 2. a 3. g 4. h 5. e 6. b 7. d 8. f; 1. auspices 2. procured 3. fluctuates 4. stolid 5. chronic 6. attrition 7. omniscient 8. palpable

Questions: 1. Tom thinks that his summer is getting off to a terrible start because he becomes sick with measles and a religious revival leaves him temporarily as the only "sinner" in town. 2. Tom and Huck feel guilty because they do not feel worthy of Muff Potter's praise. They have not revealed the information that would free Muff Potter, that they had witnessed Injun Joe kill Dr. Robinson. 3. Although Tom is exalted by all of the townspeople, he suffers feelings of insecurity after the trial because Injun Joe remains at large and may return to cause him harm. 4. The two boys begin their hole-digging project in response to Tom's questionable assumption that treasure has been hidden in town over the years by robbers. 5. It is clear that Tom and Huck are no longer afraid of Injun Joe because they are unwilling to pass up an exciting midnight excursion. 6. Tom and Huck change their plans about going to the haunted house when they suddenly realize it is Friday, a noted bad luck day. They play Robin Hood instead of going to the haunted house. 7. Injun Joe and his companion are glad they had used the haunted house as a hide-away after they discover hidden treasure in the place they were going to store their stash. 8. Dreaming of wealth, Tom and Huck decide to track Injun Joe to find the hiding place where he will store his stash and the treasure he found in the haunted house. 9. Tom is pleased when he hears that Judge Thatcher has returned because he will be able to spend time with his daughter Becky and attend her picnic. 10. Injun Joe is planning an act of revenge against Widow Douglas because her husband, as justice of the peace, had punished him publicly for illegal acts and misbehavior. 11. When Injun Joe and his companion return, Huck thinks it is better to follow them, instead of risking losing them while he follows the plan to inform Tom.

Chapters 30 – 35

Vocabulary: 1. boding–portending, fortelling 2. lucid–clear 3. sinuous–winding; twisting 4. moiety–half; share 5. forlorn–unhappy; miserable 6. insipid–dull 7. plausible–believable 8. underground

Questions: 1. Tom shows his maturity when he attempts to preserve the life of the candles; he insists that he and Becky stay by the water; and he uses the kite line to explore possible means of escape. Most of all, he remains calm and level-headed and tries to maintain good spirits in himself and Becky. 2. Tom panics when he learns that the entrance to the cave had been sealed off because he knows that Injun Joe is trapped inside. 3. Tom has mixed emotions about Injun Joe's death: he is sad when he empathizes with the suffering that must have preceded his death, but glad that he will no longer have the threat of Injun Joe's revenge hanging over him. 4. Tom wants Huck to go back into the cave with him because he knows that Injun Joe must have left the treasure behind: he expects to be able to retrieve it with Huck's assistance. 5. This time Tom brings matches, kite string, food, and bags to carry the treasure. The boys take along little bags to split the treasure into smaller, easier to carry loads. 6. Sid shows his mean nature when he spoils the Welshman's surprise about Huck's heroism in helping to save the Widow. 7. Tom upstages the widow's surprise by announcing that he and Huck are rich and by showing her and the assembled guests the bags full of coins. The widow's offer to give Huck a home and possibly an education does not mean as much when it becomes known that Huck is independently wealthy. 8. Huck runs away from the Widow Douglas because he cannot get used to the trappings of civilized life— the routines, the need to be clean and neat, to eat properly, to sleep in a bed, to attend church, etc. 9. Tom promises Huck membership in the Robber Gang if he returns to the Widow.